How To Stop Being Passive Aggressive

The Ultimate Guide on How to Not be Passive Aggressive

Mary Peterson

Table of Contents

Chapter 1

Understanding Passive-Aggression

Passive-aggressive behavior can take many forms, but it is generally defined as nonverbal aggression that manifests itself in negative behavior. Simply put, it is when you are angry with someone but are unable or unwilling to express your feelings.

Instead of communicating honestly when you are upset, annoyed, irritated, or disappointed, you may choose to bottle up your emotions. Perhaps you shut down verbally, give angry looks, make obvious behavioral changes, be obstructive, sulky, or build a stone wall. It may also include indirectly resisting requests from others by avoiding or confusing the issue, or refusing to comply. It can be either subtle and hidden or overt and obvious.

A passive-aggressive may not always express anger or resentment. They could come across as pleasant, courteous, amiable, grounded, compassionate, and well-intentioned. However, underneath, manipulation may be taking place, hence the term 'passive-aggressive'.

Passive aggression is a destructive pattern of behavior that can be interpreted as a form of emotional abuse in relationships, eroding people's trust.

It is a manifestation of negative energy 'in the ether' that is visible to all parties involved and has the potential to cause significant harm and pain. It occurs when negative emotions and feelings accumulate and are then held in by a self-imposed need for either acceptance by another, reliance on others, or the avoidance of further arguments or conflicts.

If some of this sounds familiar, don't worry; we all do some of the things listed above on occasion. It does not necessarily make us passive-aggressive, nor does it imply that your partner is. Passive aggression occurs when behavior is more persistent and repeated on a regular basis, and there are ongoing patterns of negative attitudes and passive resistance in personal relationships or at work.

Passive aggression may be viewed as a self-defense mechanism. It could be automatic or the result of early experiences. What they are protecting themselves from is unique to each individual, but it may include underlying feelings of rejection, fear, mistrust, insecurity, and/or low self-esteem.

In the workplace, a passive-aggressive employee or employer may use these techniques to exert control and/or intimidation. When given jobs to do, the worker may sulk, make faces, scowl inwardly, or agree politely but then take a long time to complete them. They are expressing annoyance in the hope that they will not be asked to do those tasks again.

Employers can also use passive aggression when confronted with employee problems, such as turning a blind eye, refusing to confront facts, or dealing with genuine cases of bullying and harassment. This avoidant behavior can be extremely harmful to individuals and groups of people within organizations.

When someone is passive-aggressive, it can harm their relationships. Because they do not openly express their emotions, those with whom they interact may not understand why they are given silent treatment or why their requests are ignored. This causes confusion about what is happening.

These behaviors can have a negative impact on the relationship over time. The passive-aggressive person's partner may grow tired of repeatedly asking for something, or they may begin to resent the sarcastic responses. This can form a wedge.

Furthermore, because the passive-aggressive person does not express their feelings, any underlying anger or frustration is never addressed. The situation worsens rather than being resolved and moving forward.

Passive-aggressive employees may face disciplinary action or even termination. A passive-aggressive student may receive low grades in school due to missed or late assignments, lowering their grades and resulting in poor academic performance.

Recognizing Passive Aggressive Behavior

For example, a person engaged in overt aggression may attend a family gathering and be rude or hostile, whereas a person engaged in passive aggression may avoid the family gathering entirely or attend and give people the "silent treatment.

Passive aggression is frequently vindictive. A person may use this communication style in retaliation for a perceived slight. Psychotherapy can help people who are struggling with passive-aggressive behavior. Several instances of passive-aggressive conduct are as follows:

Silence
The silent treatment allows you to punish someone else without actually doing anything. They may completely ignore calls or emails, refuse to talk about specific topics, or withdraw selectively from time to time.

Negative comment
Passive aggression often takes the form of subtle digs or negative comments. For example, a person may make a comment about a topic that they know makes another person uncomfortable, such as their dating history or weight.

They may also use their knowledge of a person's past to subtly harm them. A parent who struggled to sleep in their own room as a child may make negative comments about their child in relation to other children who cannot sleep independently in adulthood. In this way, they keep 'digging' at their child even years after the events described, never letting them forget and subtly putting them down.

Lateness

Most people are late on occasion, and it is not always a sign of passive aggression. In fact, this is what makes it an effective form of passive-aggression because the late person can deny being stuck in traffic or losing track of time, for example. Frequent lateness can be interpreted as disrespect. It could also be a way to avoid awkward situations or make someone feel less important. In this regard, it can be used for passive aggression.

Avoidance

People use a variety of avoidance strategies to express their aggression without being overt about it. Some examples include procrastination, avoiding returning a loved one's call, avoiding specific topics of discussion, especially if they know the other person wants to discuss those topics, and ignoring someone as a form of aggression, such as not approaching them at a party.

Weaponized kindness

People sometimes use ostensibly kind or helpful acts to express their emotions. For example, a person who is upset that a family member forgot their birthday may then "go the extra mile" to celebrate that person's birthday, then make comments about how they could never ignore such a significant occasion.

Sarcasm

Sarcasm occurs when someone says something they don't mean. Sarcasm can be used to punish others in a passive-aggressive manner. For example, they may sarcastically mock a loved one's emotions or personality traits.

Weaponized incompetence

Weaponized incompetence occurs when someone pretends to be incompetent in order to avoid an unpleasant task or punish another person. For example, a spouse may pretend to be unable to clean the bathroom or do an objectively inferior job styling a child's hair in order to avoid having to do so again.

Risks and Danger

Passive aggression is still aggression. A 2018 study of nurses discovered that people who use this style of aggression may feel just as aggressive as those who use other forms of aggression. Researchers discovered similar effects to other types of aggression, such as emotional stress. Passive aggression poses several risks, including:

Suspicion and distrust
According to the nurses in the 2018 study, passive aggression erodes trust. This could be due in part to the difficulty of directly addressing passive aggression, which has the potential to erode team cohesion.

Stress
Passive aggression can be just as stressful as other types of aggression. A person may also experience stress as a result of their inability to recognize or respond appropriately to aggression.

Relationship problems
Passive aggression masks an individual's aggressive intent, making it more difficult for those they care about to recognize and respond to their emotions. Furthermore, the desire to express aggression without communication or accountability can gradually harm relationships.

Poor communication
Passive aggression is defined as the attempt to avoid directly communicating one's emotions. This can have a negative impact on relationship communication, particularly when someone denies their aggressive intent.

Increased aggression

A person's response to passive aggression can be more passive aggression or overt aggression.

Poor mental health

Passive aggression can be a sign of and contribute to poor mental health. Passive aggression can cause high levels of stress. Passive aggression has also been linked to mental health conditions like anorexia nervosa, borderline personality, and adjustment disorders.

The Consequences of Passive-Aggressive Behavior

Passive-aggressive behavior can have far-reaching consequences, affecting many areas of life. Understanding these consequences is critical for mitigating their impact and promoting healthier interactions.

Personal Relationships

Passive-aggressive behavior can strain personal relationships, resulting in a toxic environment of resentment, mistrust, and confusion. Because of its indirect nature, underlying hostility can be difficult to address, preventing conflict resolution and impeding the development of strong emotional connections.

Professional relationships

Passive-aggressive behavior in professional settings can impede effective teamwork, stifle creativity and productivity, and create a hostile work environment. It undermines trust and communication, two critical components of effective professional relationships.

Mental Health Impact

Individuals who engage in passive-aggressive behavior on a regular basis, as well as those who are frequently the target, may experience a variety of mental health issues. This behavior is linked to chronic stress, anxiety, and depression. The ambiguity of passive aggression can cause a constant state of tension and unease, which can have a negative impact on mental health over time.

Physical Health Impact
Chronic stress and anxiety caused by passive-aggressive behavior can have a negative impact on one's physical health. Cardiovascular problems, weakened immune responses, sleep disorders, and other stress-related conditions are all possibilities.

Legal Implications
Passive-aggressive behavior may have legal consequences in certain situations. For example, in the workplace, consistent passive-aggressive behavior can be considered harassment or contribute to a hostile work environment, which can result in legal consequences.

Understanding these consequences allows us to better understand the importance of addressing passive-aggressive behavior and promoting healthier communication styles.

Chapter 2

The Causes of Passive Aggression

Those who have survived tragedies frequently resort to passive aggression. In such cases, passive aggression results from a loss of control and power. The true causes of passive aggression vary from person to person, but identifying the causes makes treating passive aggression much easier. Possible explanations for passive-aggressive behavior in social settings.

Family History
A dysfunctional family causes a variety of issues, including passive-aggressive behavior. Controlling and domineering parents frequently encourage passive-aggressive behavior in their children, particularly when there is competition for affection and attention.

Was there any back and forth with a parent about conformity and obedience? How did it affect their individual identities? Untreated passive aggression from childhood almost always persists into adulthood.

Workplace Dynamics
Interpersonal relationships at work can lead to passive-aggressive behavior, particularly in environments with high levels of competition or conflict, a lack of conflict resolution mechanisms, or a culture that discourages open expression of disagreement.

Modeling
If you are passive-aggressive, it is not surprising that your child may replicate your conduct. Children have a tendency to emulate their parents' habits, and if they realize that passive aggression is an effective strategy to demand attention and get their way, they will follow suit.

Stressful settings

Individuals may adopt passive-aggressive behavior as a coping method in difficult events or places. This is especially true when the person feels powerless or unwilling to communicate their frustration or discontent openly.

Cowardice

Not in the sense of avoiding picking battles, but in their inability to accept responsibility for their acts. Passive aggressive persons are unwilling to approach their victims or see them react to the anguish they have caused on them. They would rather blame the victims or convince them that they are the cause of whatever transpired.

Social inadequacy during the formative years

People with chronic passive aggressiveness usually experience emotions of powerlessness and social weakness throughout their earliest years. A youngster with domineering parents who consistently fails to advocate for oneself is more prone to engage in passive aggression. The same is true for children and teenagers who are continually evaluated by their peers for their physical appearance, lack of ability, and so on.

Unmanageable duties

Those who grew up with highly demanding parents and are unable to easily disagree with their outrageous expectations frequently create various ways to resist; they resist in subtle ways that others may mistake for passive-aggressive tendencies.

If we grew up in a home that didn't appreciate our basic needs and wants, our natural drive to assert ourselves was restrained.

This is typical among first-born children; the parents expect the oldest to complete more extra work than he or she is capable of handling. Over time, the oldest learns to rely on coping techniques rather than disobeying his or her parents' requests. These methods pave the way for core passive-aggressive conduct later in life, which can be directed at anyone, including a spouse, supervisor, or instructor.

Limitations on freedom of expression
When people are unable to express themselves, they can only resort to passive aggressiveness. Passive-aggressive conduct is provoked by homophobia, gender bias, discrimination, and other social constraints.

When people feel powerless in stressful situations, they resort to passive hostility. If individuals are exposed to a bad atmosphere for an extended period of time, passive aggressiveness gets entrenched and remains with them even after they leave the hostile environment.

Other Factors

Passive-aggressive behavior is a complicated phenomenon with psychological and biological reasons. Understanding these effects offers us a thorough picture of what generates this type of behavior.

Psychological Factors
Several psychological theories give light on how passive-aggressive behavior develops:

Psychoanalytic theory
This shows that passive-aggressive behavior may come from unresolved childhood problems or suppressed emotions.

Cognitive Behavioral Theory
According to this idea, passive-aggressive behavior is a learned coping mechanism acquired in situations where direct expression of anger is discouraged.

Social Learning Theory
Based on the concept of behavioral modeling, this theory claims that individuals might develop passive-aggressive behaviors by studying and imitating significant figures in their lives.

Aside from these hypotheses, specific psychiatric problems are usually related to passive-aggressive behavior:

Personality Disorders
Passive-aggressive behavior is usually related to various personality disorders, most notably Passive-Aggressive (Negativistic) Personality Disorder. People with this syndrome may feel significant resentment for others and display it through passive resistance, procrastination, stubbornness, and forgetfulness.

Depression
People suffering from depression may exhibit passive-aggressive conduct as a means of expressing despondency or dissatisfaction without engaging in direct conflict.

Anxiety
Passive-aggressive behavior may be utilized by people with anxiety disorders to avoid direct confrontations that they feel may trigger anxiety or panic.

Biological Factors
Biological considerations provide another layer of insight into what causes passive-aggressive conduct. While these elements require greater scientific inquiry, some essential factors include:

Genetics
Some research implies that our genetic makeup may influence our proclivity for passive-aggressive behavior. If passive-aggressive qualities may be inherited, it means that some people are genetically predisposed to this type of conduct.

Brain Structure and Function
Certain regions in the brain are associated with emotion management and impulse control. If these structures or functions are disrupted for any cause, including heredity, injuries, or other circumstances, the chance of passive-aggressive conduct may increase.

<u>*Hormonal influences*</u>
Hormones are chemical messengers that control numerous physiological functions, including behavior. Imbalances in some hormones, such as those involved in stress response or mood control, may contribute to passive-aggressive behavior.

<u>*Neurotransmitters*</u>
Neurotransmitters serve a vital function in communicating between nerve cells in the brain. Imbalances in neurotransmitters, such as serotonin, dopamine, or norepinephrine, may influence behavior, including the predisposition for passive-aggressive replies.

We can acquire a better understanding of what causes passive-aggressive conduct by combining our knowledge of psychology, the environment, and biology.

Recognizing Your Own Passive Aggressive Behaviors

Passive-aggressive conduct can be detrimental both when directed at us and when we show it ourselves. Recognizing and accepting your own passive-aggressive traits is vital for enhancing communication and relationships. Identifying these habits inside oneself might be challenging because they are typically subtle and arise from a desire to avoid direct disagreement.

However, being honest and self-reflective allows you to better understand your own motivations and work toward healthy communication and emotional expression. Taking responsibility for your passive-aggressive tendencies enables you to make positive adjustments and develop more open and honest relationships.

Chapter 3

The Communication Breakdown

Communication is the lifeblood of our interactions with others and an essential component of human connection. It has a significant impact on our happiness, personal development, and relationships. Effective communication allows us to express our thoughts, feelings and needs while also promoting understanding and empathy. In contrast, poor communication can result in misunderstandings, conflicts, and strained relationships.

Understanding these communication styles is essential for improving our interactions and relationships. We'll look at four primary communication styles, including their characteristics, impact, and strategies for improving communication.

The Value of Effective Communication

Before we get into the specifics of communication styles, we should emphasize the importance of effective communication in our lives and relationships. Communication is a multifaceted tool that serves a variety of important functions:

Expressing Needs
It allows us to express our needs, desires, and emotions, which helps others understand us better.

Building Relationships
Effective communication promotes deeper connections and intimacy in personal relationships, both romantic and friendship.

Conflict Resolution
It provides a means of navigating conflicts, finding common ground, and reaching agreements.

Professional Success
Strong communication skills are essential in the workplace, promoting career advancement and teamwork.

Emotional Wellbeing
Open and honest communication is closely related to emotional and mental health.

Given its broad implications, it's clear that mastering effective communication is a necessary life skill. To begin, let's look at the four main communication styles: passive, passive-aggressive, aggressive, and assertive.

Passive Communication

Features of Passive Communication:

- ➤ *Individuals frequently prioritize other people's needs and opinions over their own.*
- ➤ *Reluctance to communicate personal needs, desires, or emotions.*
- ➤ *A desire to avoid confrontation and conflict.*
- ➤ *Setting boundaries and saying "no" are difficult.*
- ➤ *Feelings of frustration, resentment, and being ignored.*

Impact of Passive Communication
Passive communication may result in unmet needs, unexpressed feelings, and unresolved conflicts. Over time, this style can erode self-esteem and impede personal development. Passive communicators may feel taken advantage of or undervalued, which frequently leads to imbalanced relationships.

Strategies to Improve Passive Communication:

- ➤ *Develop self-awareness by identifying your needs and emotions.*
- ➤ *Work on assertiveness skills, such as expressing your thoughts and feelings clearly and respectfully.*

➤ *Set and communicate boundaries with others.*
➤ *Seek out opportunities to express your thoughts and desires in everyday interactions.*

Passive-aggressive Communication

Features of Passive-Aggressive Communication:

➤ *True feelings and needs are concealed behind a passive exterior.*
➤ *Using indirect, manipulative behaviors to express anger or frustration.*
➤ *Using sarcasm, backhanded compliments, or sabotage to express displeasure.*
➤ *A desire to retain control or power in the relationship.*
➤ *Frequently accompanied by feelings of resentment and concealed anger.*

The impact of passive-aggressive communication

Passive-aggressive communication can cause confusion, misinterpretation, and ongoing conflict in relationships. It undermines trust and creates an unhealthy environment of uncertainty and instability. Over time, this style can cause irreversible damage to relationships.

Strategies for Improving Passive Aggressive Communication:

➤ *Develop self-awareness and recognize underlying emotions.*
➤ *When expressing needs or concerns, communicate openly and directly.*
➤ *Create healthier ways to deal with anger and frustration.*
➤ *Seek professional help if passive-aggressive behaviors continue.*

Aggressive communication

Characteristics of Aggressive Communication:

- ➢ *Dominating conversations and attempting to shape the narrative.*
- ➢ *A strong desire to be correct, frequently dismissing other people's perspectives.*
- ➢ *Frequent use of harsh language, yelling, or intimidation.*
- ➢ *Difficulty listening to opposing views.*
- ➢ *Conflicts tend to escalate instead of being resolved.*

The Impact of Aggressive Communication

Aggressive communication can cause fear, hostility, and emotional harm in relationships. It frequently leads to a power struggle, in which one person's opinions and needs take precedence over the other's, leaving the latter feeling ignored and disrespected. Aggressive communication can undermine trust and prevent effective problem-solving.

Strategies to Improve Aggressive Communication:

- ➢ *Active listening involves taking into account the perspectives of others.*
- ➢ *Develop empathy and an understanding of different points of view.*
- ➢ *Develop anger management skills so you can express your frustration constructively.*
- ➢ *Learn conflict resolution strategies that encourage collaboration.*

Assertive Communication

Characteristics of assertive communication:

- ➢ *Clear and respectful communication of thoughts, feelings, and needs.*
- ➢ *A willingness to actively listen to others.*
- ➢ *Be open to feedback and constructive criticism.*
- ➢ *A focus on collaboration and mutual respect.*
- ➢ *Being able to set and uphold proper boundaries.*

The impact of assertive communication

Assertive communication fosters healthy relationships based on trust, respect, and clear communication. It creates an atmosphere in which all parties feel valued and heard, resulting in better conflict resolution and mutual understanding.

Strategies for developing assertive communication:

> *Develop self-awareness to identify your own needs and emotions.*
> *Develop active listening skills in order to effectively communicate with others.*
> *Use "I" statements to express emotions and thoughts without blaming or accusing.*
> *Set and communicate boundaries with clarity and respect.*
> *Seek assertiveness training or therapy to improve communication skills.*

Intersection of Communication Styles and Relationships

Our chosen communication style has a significant impact on our relationships. In many cases, couples' communication styles differ, which can lead to conflicts and challenges. Let's look at how the interplay of these styles affects relationships.

Passive and aggressive dynamics

Power imbalances and conflicts are common in relationships where one communicator is passive and the other is aggressive. The passive person may feel overwhelmed or undervalued, whereas the aggressive partner may experience a lack of empathy.

Passive and passive-aggressive dynamics

This combination can result in suppressed emotions and unspoken conflicts within a relationship. Resentment can build over time, resulting in a tense and unhealthy atmosphere.

Aggressive and passive-aggressive dynamics

These dynamics can lead to explosive conflicts and emotional harm. Both individuals may use manipulative tactics, making it difficult to resolve issues constructively.

Assertive communication in relationships:

Relationships with assertive communication tend to be happier and more satisfying. Both partners feel heard and respected, conflicts are discussed openly, and collaborative problem-solving is more likely.

Improve Communication Skills for Stronger Relationships

Improving your communication skills is a worthwhile endeavor that can have a significant impact on your relationships and general well-being. Here are some practical steps for improving your communication:

Self-Awareness

Begin by understanding your own communication style, including its strengths and weaknesses. Recognize your emotions, needs, and triggers in different situations.

Active Listening

Active listening involves paying full attention to the speaker, asking clarifying questions, and reflecting on what you've heard. This promotes mutual understanding.

Empathy

Develop empathy by attempting to understand situations from the perspective of others. Empathetic responses validate emotions and foster connections.

Healthy boundaries

Set and communicate your boundaries concisely and respectfully. Encourage others to do the same while respecting their personal boundaries.

Conflict Resolution
Learn conflict-resolution strategies that emphasize collaboration and problem-solving. Avoid the blame game and concentrate on solutions.

Seek feedback
Request feedback from trusted friends, family, or a therapist to better understand your communication style and areas for improvement.

Relationships that are fulfilling and healthy are built on effective communication. Understanding and refining your communication style allows you to strengthen relationships, resolve conflicts, and promote personal growth. Whether your communication style is passive, passive-aggressive, or aggressive, you can make the transition to assertive communication.

Practicing communication skills improves not only your relationships but also your overall quality of life. Remember that interaction is a lifelong learning process, and with practice and dedication, you can improve your interactions and form deeper connections with others.

Chapter 4

Emotional Intelligence

Emotional intelligence improves your performance in the workplace and in your personal life, but it all begins with you. Understanding and managing your own emotions can boost your confidence, empathy, and optimism, as well as your social skills and self-control.

Regardless of your professional field, whether you manage a team of two or twenty, or even just yourself, understanding how effective you are at managing your own emotional energy is a great place to start. Emotional intelligence is not taught or tested in the curriculum, so where did it come from, what is it, do you have it, and how important is it?

Simply put, Emotional Intelligence is the ability to identify and manage one's own emotions as well as respond to the emotions of others. Understanding how your emotions shape your thoughts and actions allows you to gain more control over your behavior and develop the skills you need to manage yourself more effectively. Becoming more emotionally conscious allows us to mature and gain a better understanding of who we are, allowing us to communicate more effectively with others and form stronger bonds. These pointers will help you get started on discovering the foundations of your emotional intelligence.

Practice observing your feelings
We often lead hectic, busy lives, and it is all too easy to lose touch with our emotions. To reconnect, try setting a timer for various times throughout the day. When the timer goes off, take a few deep breaths and assess your emotional state. Pay attention to where that emotion manifests as a physical feeling in your body, as well as how the sensation feels. With consistent practices, it will become second nature to you.

Pay attention to your behavior
While practicing emotional awareness, take the time to observe your own behavior. Examine how you behave when you are experiencing certain emotions and how this affects your day-to-day activities. Managing our emotions becomes easier as we become more aware of how we respond to them.

Question your own opinions
In today's hyper-connected world, it is easy to become trapped in an 'opinion bubble'. This is a state of being in which your own beliefs are constantly reinforced by others who hold similar views. Take the time to read the other side of the story and have your perspectives challenged, even if you still believe they are correct. This will help you understand others and be more open to new ideas.

Accept responsibility for your feelings
Your emotions and behavior are entirely your own; once you accept responsibility for how you feel and behave, it will have a positive impact on all aspects of your life.

Take time to celebrate the positives
Celebrating and reflecting on positive life experiences is an important aspect of emotional intelligence. People who experience positive emotions are more resilient and more likely to have satisfying relationships, which will aid them in overcoming adversity.

But do not ignore the negative
Reflecting on negative feelings is equally important as reflecting on positive ones. Understanding why you feel negative is critical to becoming a well-rounded individual who can deal with negative situations in the future.

Do not forget to breathe
Life throws us a variety of situations, and most of us deal with stress on a regular basis. Remember to breathe if you want to manage your emotions and avoid outbursts. Call a time-out and go splash some cold water on your face, go outside for some fresh air, or make a

drink - anything to keep your cool and give yourself time to figure out
what's going on and how you should react.

A lifelong process
Understand and remember that emotional intelligence is something
you can develop and improve over time; it is a lifelong practice.

Self-awareness
Self-awareness, a key component of emotional intelligence, is the
ability to recognize and understand your own personality, moods,
and emotions, as well as how they affect others. It entails conducting
a realistic self-assessment of your capabilities, strengths, and
weaknesses, and understanding how others perceive you. It can
help you identify areas for self-improvement, improve your
adaptability, and limit mistakes.

Learn to see yourself objectively
Knowing yourself completely is difficult, and it is nearly impossible to
look at yourself objectively, so feedback from those who know you is
crucial. Ask them about your strengths and weaknesses, record their
responses, and compare them. Look for patterns and remember not
to argue with them; it doesn't mean they're correct; they're simply
attempting to help you gauge your perception from another's point of
view.

Keep a diary
Keeping a diary is an excellent way to gain an accurate
understanding of yourself. Begin by writing down what happened to
you at the end of each day, how you felt, and how you handled it.
Documenting such details will increase your awareness of what
you're doing and highlight potential sources of problems. Examine
your comments on a regular basis to identify trends.

Understand what motivates you
When starting a new project, everyone has a core motivation. When
faced with adversity, it is difficult to remember this motivator. All too
often, people begin a project but abandon it because they lose

motivation. Take the time to understand what motivates you and use it to propel you to the finish line.

Take it easy

Emotional outbursts can occur when we do not take the time to slow down and process our feelings. Give yourself a break and make a conscious effort to meditate, practice yoga, or read; a little escapism can do wonders. And then, the next time you have an emotional reaction to something, try to pause before responding.

Identify your emotional triggers

Self-aware people are able to recognize their emotions as they happen. It is critical to be flexible with your emotions and adjust them to your circumstances. Don't deny your emotions at this stage, but don't be rigid about them either; instead, take the time to process your emotions before communicating them.

Predict how you will feel

Consider an upcoming situation and predict how you will feel. Practice naming and accepting your feelings; naming them gives you control. Instead of simply reacting to the feeling, try to choose an appropriate response.

Believe in your intuition

If you're still unsure which path to take, trust your instincts. After all, your subconscious has been determining which path to take for your entire life.

Self-management

Once you understand self-awareness and how your emotions work, you can begin to manage yourself. This includes taking responsibility for your own behavior and well-being, as well as managing emotional outbursts.

Snap out of it

Changing your sensory input is an important way to keep your emotions under control; as the old saying goes, motion dictates emotion. So, jolt your physical body out of routine by taking an exercise class, or try to channel a busy mind with a puzzle or a book, anything to break your current routine.

Maintain a schedule
If you want to complete tasks efficiently, you must create and adhere to a schedule.

When you schedule appointments on your calendar, you're telling yourself, "I'm going to do A, B, and C by X date and it'll take Y hours." When you make this promise, it becomes more difficult to procrastinate.

Eat well
This sounds simple, but controlling what you eat and drink can have a significant impact on your emotional state, so do your best to maintain a balanced diet.

Don't be mad
Direct your emotional energy into something productive. It is acceptable to keep overwhelming emotions inside, especially if it is not the appropriate time to express them. However, instead of venting your frustration on something futile, use it to motivate yourself. Don't be angry; instead, strive to improve.

Become interested
A key factor in managing yourself and your emotions is making a conscious effort to be interested in the subject matter, whether it is business or personal.

Trusting
Establishing trust with someone can be difficult, and once lost, it is extremely difficult to regain. Try to remember that people are only human and will make mistakes. By demonstrating your trustworthiness, you invite others to reciprocate.

It's your choice
You have the ability to choose how you respond to a situation; you can overreact or remain calm. But the choice is yours.

Motivation
Self-motivation, a personal skills component of emotional intelligence, refers to our inner drive to achieve and improve our commitment to our goals, our willingness to act on opportunities, and our overall optimism.

Personal Goals
Personal goals can provide both long-term guidance and short-term motivation. So grab a pen and paper, think about where you want to be, and set some goals for yourself. Based on your strengths, make them relevant to you, and finally, make them exciting and attainable. This task alone will instantly motivate you!

Be realistic
When you set a new goal, make sure to give yourself realistic and specific goals for achieving it, and remember that change is an unavoidable part of life. Achievement boosts confidence, and as self-confidence grows, so does the ability to achieve more. Can you see how this works?

Positive thinking
To stay motivated, it's essential to maintain a positive and optimistic attitude. See problems and setbacks as learning opportunities rather than failures, and avoid negative people in favor of positive, well-motivated people; they will have a positive impact on you.

Lifelong learning
Both knowledge and information are essential for keeping your mind stimulated and motivated. And with information so easily accessible, you can fuel your values and passions with the click of a button!

Comfort Zone
The biggest impediment to reaching your full potential is not challenging yourself enough. If you're willing to step outside of your comfort zone, you can achieve great things, so do it as often as possible.

Help

Don't be afraid to ask for assistance when you need it, and vice versa. If someone else requires assistance, don't hesitate to provide it. Seeing others succeed will only serve to motivate you.

Stand and stretch

Take a stand and stretch out as far as you can for 10 seconds to give yourself a quick boost of motivation. When you return to your desk, you will be in the right frame of mind and prepared to work.

Empathy

Simply put, empathy is the ability to understand another person's emotions. Recognize that everyone has their own set of emotions, desires, triggers, and fears. Empathy involves allowing their experiences to connect with your own in order to respond in an emotionally suitable manner. It's a lifelong skill and the most crucial one for navigating relationships, and while it doesn't come naturally, there are a few ways to cultivate it.

Listen

Before you can empathize with someone, you must first understand what they are saying, so listening is at the heart of empathy. It entails allowing them to speak without interruption, preconceptions, or skepticism, and putting your own problems on hold so that you can absorb their situation and consider how they are feeling before reacting.

Try to be approachable

Whether you're leading a team or working on a project with others, try to stay accessible and approachable.

Perspective

We've all heard the phrase "put yourself in their shoes," and this is exactly that. The simplest way to gain some perspective the next time an issue or situation arises is to put yourself in the shoes of the other person and truly consider what is going on from their perspective. Sometimes there is no right or wrong answer, but you will understand enough to reach a conclusion or provide useful advice.

Open yourself up
One of the quickest ways to offer a genuine exchange or demonstrate empathy is to listen to someone's experiences and relate them to your own. Don't be afraid to open up; it could be the beginning of a wonderful and long-lasting friendship.

Immerse yourself in a new culture
Even in today's shrinking world, the old adage 'travel broadens the mind' remains true. Sometimes the best way to clear your mind is to hop on a plane and travel somewhere completely different.

Cultivate curiosity about strangers
People with high empathy levels are insatiably curious about strangers. When we talk to people outside of our usual social circle, we learn about and begin to understand different perspectives, opinions, and lives. Next time you're on a bus, you'll know exactly what to do.

Acknowledge what people are saying
Another helpful tip is to use acknowledgment words such as 'I understand' and 'I see' to demonstrate that you are listening, but only if you are truly listening.

Social skills
In terms of emotional intelligence, social skills are the abilities required to effectively manage and influence the emotions of others. It encompasses a wide range of skills, from communication and conflict resolution to dealing with change, meeting new people, and developing relationships, and it plays a role in almost every aspect of our lives, from friendship to romance and work. It's complicated and requires almost every point we've already mentioned, but here are a few pointers for you.

Get started

A good way to get started to enhance your social skills is to isolate one skill that you know you want to improve; this narrows it down and gives you direction. Daniel Goleman, an internationally known psychologist, suggests focusing on someone you know who excels at that skill, observing how they act and control their emotions, and then implementing and applying that knowledge to yourself.

Practice makes perfect

The concept of practicing your social skills may seem strange, but like everything else in life, practice makes perfect.

Stop using social media completely

We don't mean to sound old, but taking your social life offline and engaging with people in person will provide you with numerous opportunities to learn and improve your social skills. So, instead of instant messaging your best friend, arrange to meet up for a drink! Emotional intelligence does not limit itself to social media.

Get networking

Attending local networking events is a great way to improve your social skills. The great thing about these events is that everyone who attends has a common reason for coming.

The manner you communicate

We're discussing the importance of nonverbal communication and how it can influence someone's opinion of you. Body language, tone of voice, and eye contact are all important ways to communicate your emotional state to others. So, once you've calmed your emotions, consider how you present yourself physically.

The unknown

The best way to improve your social skills is to get out there and be sociable. It sounds simple, but you can't improve your social skills unless you interact with others! Join a group or network outside of your usual circle; this is an excellent way to put all of our advice into practice.

What to Avoid

Those with a high EQ rarely exhibit the following characteristics, which you should be aware of.

Drama
Emotionally intelligent people listen, give sound advice, and show empathy to those in need, but they do not let other people's lives and emotions influence or rule theirs.

Complaining
Complaining implies two things: first, that we are victims; second, that there are no solutions to our problems. An emotionally intelligent person rarely feels victimized, and even fewer feel that a solution is out of reach. So, rather than looking for someone or something to blame, they think constructively and resolve the issue in private.

Negativity
Emotionally intelligent people can avoid cynical thoughts. They recognize that negative thoughts are just that: thoughts, and they rely on facts to reach conclusions, as well as the ability to silence or zone out any negativity.

Reflecting on the past
Those with high emotional intelligence choose to learn from their mistakes and choices, and instead of concentrating on the past, they attempt to live in the present.

Selfishness
While some selfishness is required to succeed in life, extreme selfishness can strain relationships and produce conflict. Try not to be overly selfish and instead consider the needs of others.

Giving into peer pressure.
They are not bound to do anything merely because everyone else is doing it. They think independently and never conform just to satisfy others.

Being too critical
Nothing reduces a person's morale faster than being overly critical.
Remember that individuals are merely human, and they share your
motives (and limits). Take the time to comprehend another individual,
and then express the desired change.

You, too, can accomplish your full potential and goals by
understanding and effectively implementing emotional intelligence.

Chapter 5

Conflict Resolution Skills

It can be highly unpleasant and detrimental to deal with a quarrel, especially while seeking to resolve it constructively. This chapter will teach you some of the most successful ways of coping with passive-aggressive conduct in a confrontation, whether it comes from your partner, friend, coworker, or yourself.

Identify the indicators
Recognizing passive-aggressive behavior is the first step toward correcting it. Signs may include giving backhanded compliments or insults, agreeing to do something but then procrastinating or doing it poorly, making excuses or blaming others for problems, giving silent treatment or retreating from conversation, and ignoring any unpleasant emotions while acting bitter or aggressive. If you see any of these traits in yourself or someone else, you're definitely dealing with passive-aggressive behavior.

Address the issue
The second step is to confront the matter directly and gently. Passive-aggressive behavior is generally motivated by a fear of confrontation, insecurity, or a lack of trust, so it is vital to provide a secure and respectful environment in order to explore the problem and underlying feelings. To do this, utilize "I" expressions to express your sentiments and wants, rather than accusing or condemning others. Instead of forming assumptions or passing judgment, ask open-ended questions to better comprehend the other person's point of view and motivations. Listen actively and empathically to the other person's response without interrupting or ignoring it. Recognize and validate the other person's emotions and worries, even if you disagree. Additionally, avoid utilizing sarcasm, irony, or passive-aggressive statements because they will simply escalate the conflict.

Set boundaries and expectations
The third stage is to establish clear and realistic boundaries and expectations for both yourself and the other person. It is vital to declare and protect your own rights and demands, as passive-aggressive behavior typically overlooks them. To accomplish this, you must be clear about what you expect from the other person and what you are ready to contribute in exchange. You can employ both positive and negative consequences to foster collaboration or discourage animosity. Furthermore, it is vital to be consistent in your words and actions, hold the other person accountable for theirs, and not allow or condone passive-aggressive behavior. This will help you keep your self-esteem and trust.

Seek aid if necessary
The final step is to seek assistance when needed. If passive-aggressive behavior is too ingrained, persistent, or detrimental to deal with on your own, you may need to seek help from a life coach, therapist, or mediator. Feeling overwhelmed, weary, or depressed by the disagreement; attempting earlier measures with little change or exacerbating the problem; or suffering from mental health concerns such as anxiety, depression, or personality disorders. Additionally, if physical, emotional, or verbal abuse is present, it is vital to get aid.

Passive-aggressive conduct can be tough to control in a confrontation, but it can be overcome. By applying these tactics, you may deal with stress more successfully and positively, thus increasing your relationships and well-being.

Chapter 6

Mindfulness and Self-care

Anger, fear, and grief have always existed in our lives and influenced how we operate, but never as much as during a global epidemic. Mindfulness is one of the most accessible strategies for dealing with tough feelings successfully.

Unfortunately, one typical mistake I hear when talking to executives about mindfulness is that it is supposed to disconnect from emotions. That is a potentially hazardous misperception; in fact, mindfulness may help us connect with our emotions and overcome the urge most of us have to avoid them. Bypassing hurts not only our health and well-being but also our relationships with others. According to a study, workers who are educated to fake their emotions are considerably more likely to encounter physical and mental health concerns.

There are three strategies humans typically utilize to escape feelings:

Suppressing
When we conceal a feeling, we push it down and set it aside. We don't want to be bothered by it and may not know what to do with it. Some sentiments may be more difficult for us to experience than others, based on the messages we've acquired culturally or from family.

Escaping
We can also try to entirely avoid the experience, usually by indulging in some type of numbing activity. Avoidance methods include drinking, watching TV, utilizing social media, and obsessively checking news or email. I recently led a workshop on mindfulness and substance abuse for a diverse group of executives from some of the largest technology companies, and all of them admitted that, despite their hectic schedules, they spent significant time and effort

escaping their emotions through some or all of the aforementioned methods.

We're taking action on it
Some executives take pride in their proclivity to act on a gut feeling, for example, by sending a reactionary, angry email rather than taking the time to think it through. Acting on a feeling in a triggering situation usually entails projecting the difficult emotion onto someone else and blaming them for our anger, sadness, or frustration. As with suppressing and escaping, hastily acting on a feeling is an attempt to avoid it.

Bypassing has several disadvantages. A bypassed feeling remains unresolved. Suppressed anger, for example, does not go away; it is either bottled up and causes us to become more aggressive, or it transforms into passive aggressiveness and gradually erodes our relationships. Feelings are frequently indicators that some action is required. For example, anger may indicate that a boundary has been crossed and must be restored, that we must advocate for a need, or that saying no is necessary. When we allow ourselves to feel our anger mindfully, we can make more conscious decisions about how to deal with it. One executive told me that after becoming more aware of her anger, she felt ready to confront her bosses' abusive behavior and was able to put an end to it.

Another example is sadness, which may indicate that we need to grieve and let go. One of the most common mistakes I see is not allowing enough time to grieve the loss of the past. Allowing ourselves, our teams, and our organizations to grieve does not imply that the old was superior; rather, it indicates that we are actively letting go in order to make way for something new.

When practiced correctly, mindfulness can help us connect with our feelings and resolve them in a productive way. Here are three strategies for dealing with your emotions before they have a negative impact on your health, career, or colleagues.

Feel your feelings without judging or controlling them. The first step toward mindfulness is to recognize what you're feeling. Many of us lack emotional literacy, and in the midst of back-to-back meetings, we frequently have no idea what emotions we're bringing to any given situation. According to research, expressing our feelings in words, the more specific the better can help to reduce the distress caused by an experience.

Throughout the day, when you notice yourself becoming frustrated, anxious, or sad, take a moment to pause. Begin by focusing on your breath, and then try to name your experience. Now locate the feeling within your body; most of us experience our emotions in specific parts of our bodies. Don't try to change it or do anything with it; just observe it. What's the sensation? When you do this, you'll notice that bodily sensations and feelings are rarely static. Your sadness may feel like pressure in your chest at first, but as you become more aware of it, it may feel like a stab in the heart.

When you stop resisting the feeling and give it your full attention, it will usually move and eventually dissipate. This approach can be a surprising paradigm shift for many of us who are not accustomed to expressing our emotions.

Drop the story, not the feeling. Our minds are thought-generating tools, and we quickly come up with a variety of explanations for our emotions, many of which revolve around blaming others for how we're feeling or constructing justifications for our emotions. Mindfulness enables us to recognize that, while external events may have triggered our emotions, it is our interpretation of those events that cause them, giving us back control. Our stories can be endless and self-reinforcing, and engaging with them usually results in more stories. In mindfulness, we learn to gradually let go of our belief in these stories. In fact, a large part of what we do in mindfulness is noticing when we are caught up in a thought and then returning to our breath.

Letting go of the story does not mean accepting the situation. In fact, it is often not until an executive is willing to drop their story and stop blaming that they are willing to face a problem head-on. When coaching executives through transitions, for example, I've frequently discovered that they must first allow themselves to feel their sadness, exhaustion, and anxiety without blaming it on circumstances or others in order to muster the courage to change course. Dropping the story, but not the emotion, allows us to approach the situation with curiosity and a willingness to learn while leveraging the energy behind the emotion can propel us into action. It allows us to shift our focus from the past to the future and the opportunities it holds.

Do not conceal, but rather reveal. Using mindfulness at the start of a meeting, followed by a simple check-in question such as "What am I feeling?" provides an excellent opportunity to share feelings with others, fostering intimacy and connection.

During a leadership team offsite I facilitated, two divisions had recently merged, resulting in a joint division with a joint leadership team. Following a mindfulness exercise, it became clear that both sides were angry, resentful, fearful, and sad about the merger. I paused the agenda and asked the team if they felt they had grieved the loss of their respective divisions. They appeared surprised; grief is not usually given much attention in organizations, but it is an important part of the change process, and they were willing to participate in a round of sharing what they thought they had lost and how they felt about it. It was an intense and emotional moment for everyone, and it served as a great bonding opportunity. When they first spoke openly about their feelings, they realized that they had all gone through similar experiences during the change.

Revealing includes discussing feelings when we are reflecting rather than in the heat of the moment. Instead of blaming the other person's actions for our unfavorable feelings, we give our perception of the person's behavior or situation and explain how we came to have those feelings.

In a recent mindfulness class I taught for a large tech business, an executive revealed that it was normal for him to talk colleagues, children, and others out of their feelings. He regularly used the dismissive statement, "there's no cause to be upset." He learned how liberating and validating it was for both him and the other person to just have their sentiments recognized. To his amazement, the simple act of acknowledging helped the other person feel more in control and less terrified. When asked how he felt about admitting a team member's anxieties, he stopped for a time before answering, "Scared".

Conclusion

If you've been accused of being passive-aggressive, you may be wondering what it means and how you may improve your conduct. Passive-aggressive behavior is an attempt to dominate or manipulate someone without being clear about your feelings or desires.

During World War II, the term "passive-aggressive" was first used clinically to describe soldiers who refused to accept leaders' directives. Examples of passive-aggressive behavior include:

Having secret expectations
Not telling someone what you want but feeling angry, sad, or offended when you don't receive it

Saying one thing and meaning another
Saying something kind in a sarcastic tone of voice, or saying anything harsh about someone while thinking it's a joke.

Giving somebody the silent treatment
Ignoring someone, refusing to answer their calls, not responding to their texts, excluding them from gatherings, saying hi to everyone except them, avoiding eye contact, or pretending not to hear them

Expressing your feelings nonverbally
Smiling or rolling your eyes when chatting with someone, or expressing your discontent by pouting, sighing excessively, or puffing

Embarrass someone
Asking someone difficult questions in front of others to put them on the spot, revealing embarrassing information about them, gossiping about them to others while they're in hearing, or informing others about concerns you have with them instead of discussing them directly

Working Against Someone
Pretending to support someone but secretly hoping things do not go their way, or actually working to undermine or sabotage them so they don't receive what they want.

Procrastinating
Taking your sweet time to do something for someone, claiming to forget you have to do it, or purposefully keeping someone waiting

Giving gifts for ulterior motives
Giving gifts that are aimed to change someone instead of appreciating them, such as purchasing them items in your style rather than theirs.

Giving Backhanded Compliments
Giving someone a cleverly veiled insult, such as "You look so good today, I didn't recognize you!" or "That hairstyle makes you more beautiful, it makes your face looks smaller"

Characteristics of Passive-Aggressive People

These are some of the traits of passive-aggressive people as contrasted to those who are more straightforward.

Passive-Aggressive:

- ★ *Expecting others to comprehend what you desire.*
- ★ *Getting irritated when things do not go your way.*
- ★ *Preventing direct confrontation at any cost.*
- ★ *Not communicating openly.*
- ★ *Wanting to manipulate others.*
- ★ *Seeing others as opponents*
- ★ *Being stubborn.*
- ★ *Refusing to admit that you could be mistaken*

People Who are More Direct:

- ★ *Simply ask for what you want.*
- ★ *Recognize that you might not always get your wish.*
- ★ *Telling someone why you are upset with them.*
- ★ *Communicating honestly and assertively.*
- ★ *Let go of things beyond your control.*
- ★ *Empathize with others*
- ★ *Being open-minded*
- ★ *Respecting other people's thoughts and perspectives*

Possible Causes of Passive-Aggression

Here are some of the possible causes of passive aggression:

Cultural Factors

Direct confrontation is considered impolite in some cultures, thus expressing tough feelings discreetly may be a more acceptable approach.

Childhood Experiences

Some youngsters grow up in situations where disputing with authority people is frowned upon, or even deadly, so they avoid conflicts as adults.

Fear of Rejection

Passive-aggressive behavior might come from uncertainty and fear of rejection. When you merely hint at something and don't ask explicitly for what you want or need, being rejected or ignored hurts a lot less.

Unrealistic Expectations

Sometimes, people assume that someone who truly understands or loves them would know what they want, so they don't want to "spoil the romance" by discussing it. Many protagonists in love stories are passive-aggressive, which can give people the notion that true love does not involve honest communication.

Passive-aggressive Personality Disorder

Passive-aggressive communication and behaviors may also be caused by passive-aggressive personality disorder (PAPD). PAPD, which is characterized by vindictiveness, can create relationship dysfunction and other interpersonal disorders.3 Although PAPD is no longer included in the DSM-5-TR, mental health practitioners may still use the term.

Ways to be less passive-aggressive.

Here are some techniques for becoming less passive-aggressive and more direct:

Develop self-awareness
Start paying attention to your own thoughts, words, and actions to discover if you're being passive-aggressive. Spend some time thinking about why you're doing it and what you genuinely desire instead.

Ask for what you want
If you simply ask for what you want, you might just receive it. For example, someone who asks for a promotion and negotiates for it is more likely to get it than someone who does not. Even if you don't get what you want, you may obtain honest feedback that will benefit you.

Improve your communication skills
It is vital to grasp how to communicate openly, honestly, and assertively. Identify those who communicate successfully and follow their lead. Reading books or enrolling in a communication class may also be beneficial.

Express your anger in healthy ways
If you're angry or unhappy about anything, learn to express it in a healthy manner.

Empathize with others
Instead of viewing others as opponents, try to understand and empathize with them.

Give up on issues that are out of your control
Think about what you should and shouldn't control. Ask yourself why you have such strong feelings about things over which you believe you have control. Learn to let go of things that you cannot control.

Create a healthy support system
Avoid people who communicate passively aggressively and instead surround yourself with people who are honest and direct. Learn how to offer and accept assistance.

Benefits of being less passive-aggressive

Life is much less dramatic when you simply ask for what you want and say what you mean. Some advantages of being less passive-aggressive include:

Improved relationships
When you ask for what you want and are clear about it, you help to foster healthier communication patterns in all of your relationships. Couples who practice effective communication, for example, report higher levels of relationship satisfaction.

Increased life satisfaction
When you can be more direct and assertive, you're more likely to get the results you want.

Increased confidence
Learning how to be more direct while remaining tactful will most likely make you feel more in control of yourself and thus more confident.

www.ingramcontent.com/pod-product-compliance
Lightning Source LLC
Chambersburg PA
CBHW071008260726
48661CB00007B/2861